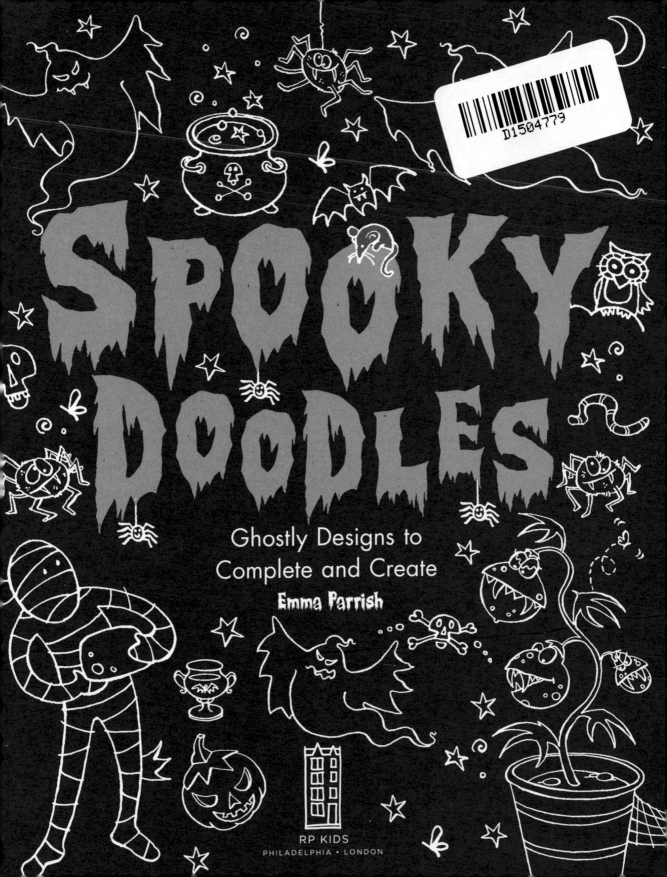

SPOOKY DOODLES

Ghostly Designs to
Complete and Create

Emma Parrish

RP KIDS

PHILADELPHIA · LONDON

First published in Great Britain by Buster Books,
an imprint of Michael O'Mara Books Limited, 2009

First published in the United States
by Running Press Book Publishers, 2010

Printed in the United States

9   8   7   6   5   4   3   2   1
Digit on the right indicates the number of this printing

ISBN 978-0-7624-3829-7

Illustrated by Emma Parrish

This edition published by Running Press Kids,
an imprint of Running Press Book Publishers
2300 Chestnut Street
Philadelphia, PA 19103-4371

Visit us on the web!
www.runningpress.com

Draw the sleepy vampire a cozy coffin bed.

What lives through here?

What can she see?

What is casting this shadow?

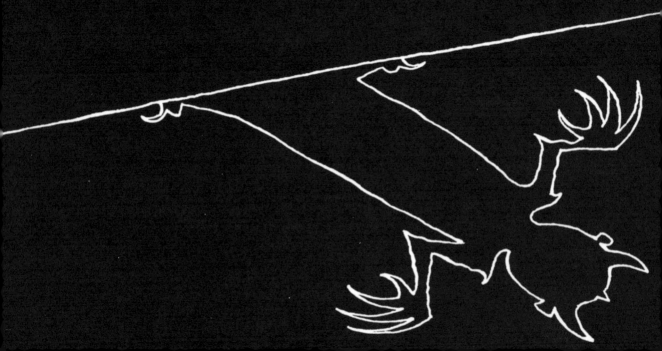

Fill the tree with bats and owls.

What are they wearing for Halloween?

Complete the cobwebs.

What is on the monsters' menu?

MENU

Draw the witches at the meeting.

A wedding feast for the newlyweds!

Who was sleeping in the coffin?

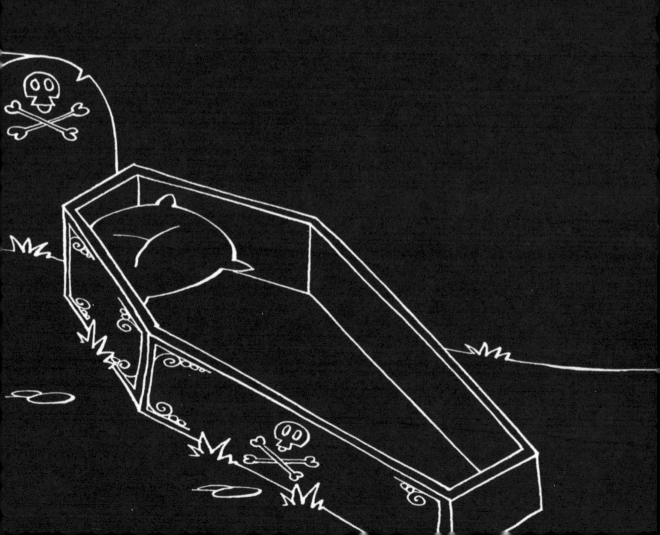

Complete Frankenstein's machine.

Design my cloak.

Who is traveling to
the Ghosts' Ball?

Decorate the room for a Halloween party.

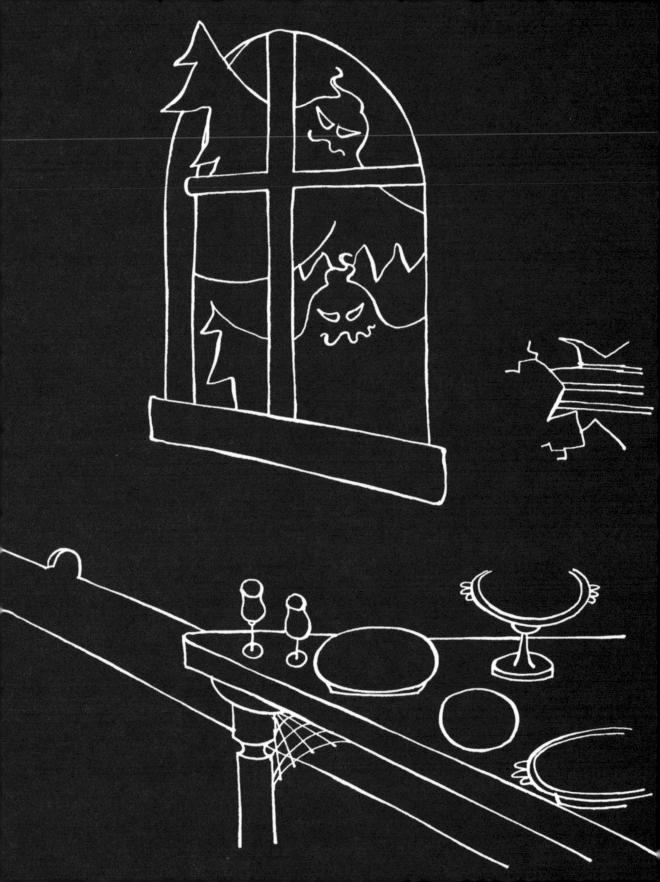

Finish the haunted house on the hill.

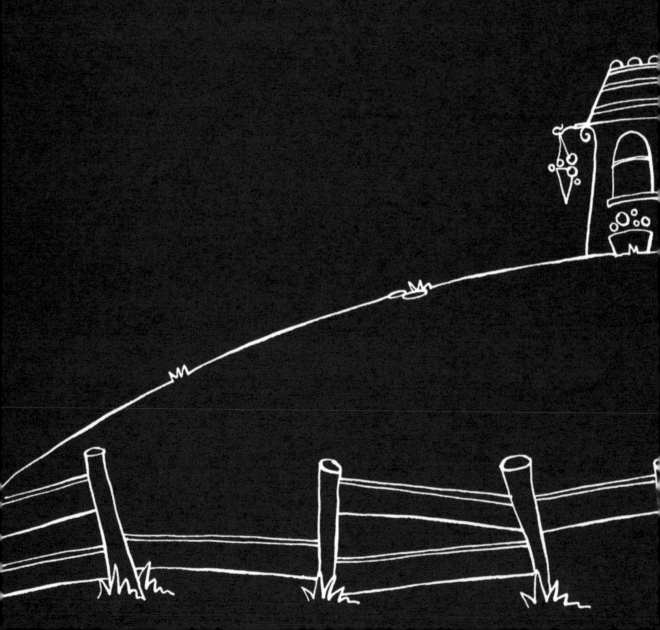

What do skeletons eat for breakfast?

Give the witch a scary manicure.

What is the mad scientist making?

Draw the keys to unlock the castle.

Create an Ice-Scream Sundae!

What goes bump
in the attic?

What is flying across the moon tonight?

Stack the pumpkins in the shop.

Is the monster happy or angry to see you?

Who is at the door?

Give the witch
more warts.

Where are these ghosts haunting?

Build the mummy a pyramid to rest in.

Write a coded message in spooky symbols.

Who is creeping up the stairs?

It's the witching hour...

Fill the window with pumpkin lanterns.

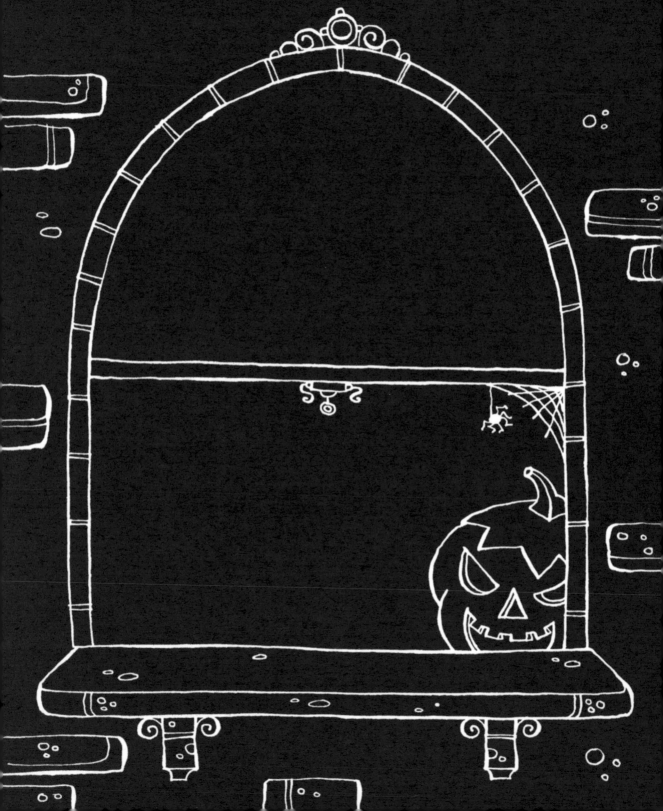

Draw the witch's real reflection.

Whose footprints are these?

Give the spiders legs.

Who won the fancy-dress competition?

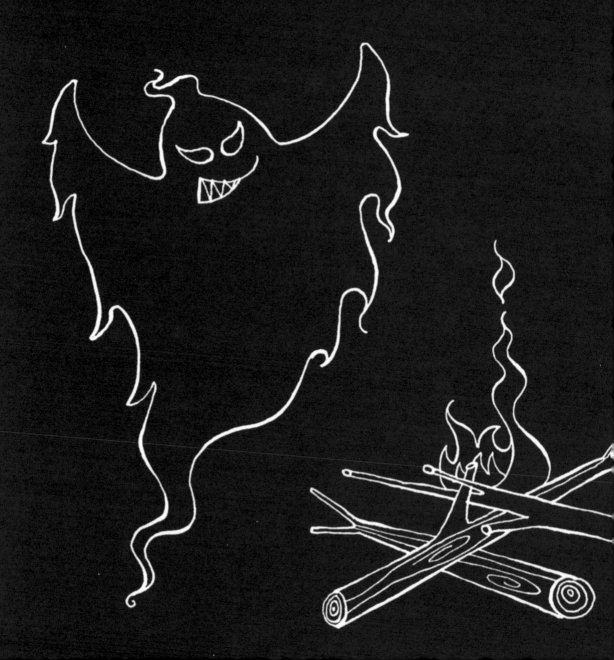

Give these ghouls a bonfire
to dance around.

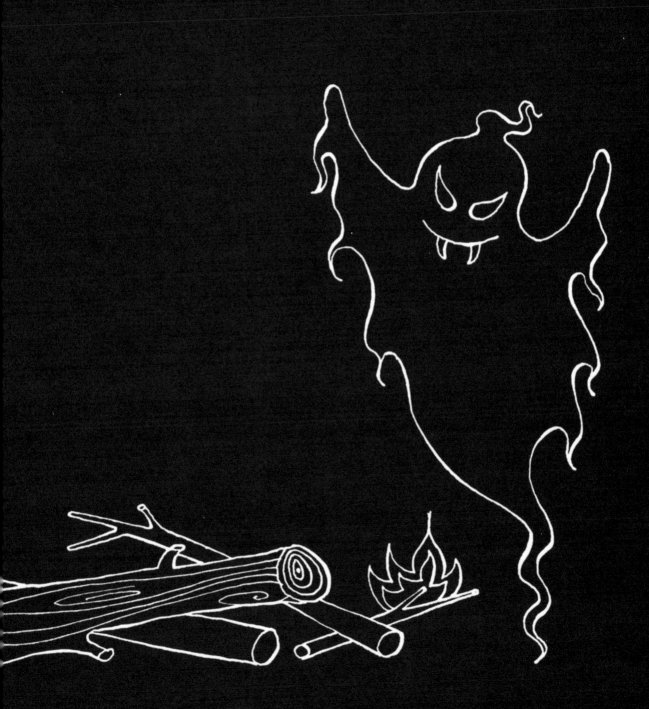

Finish the zombie bride's dress.

What did they conjure up?

Who is hiding in the basement?

Make this scene seriously spooky.

Grow a monster garden.

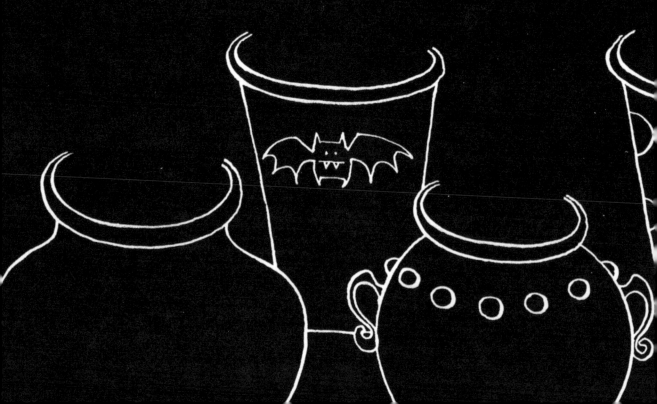

Decorate the wizards' wands.

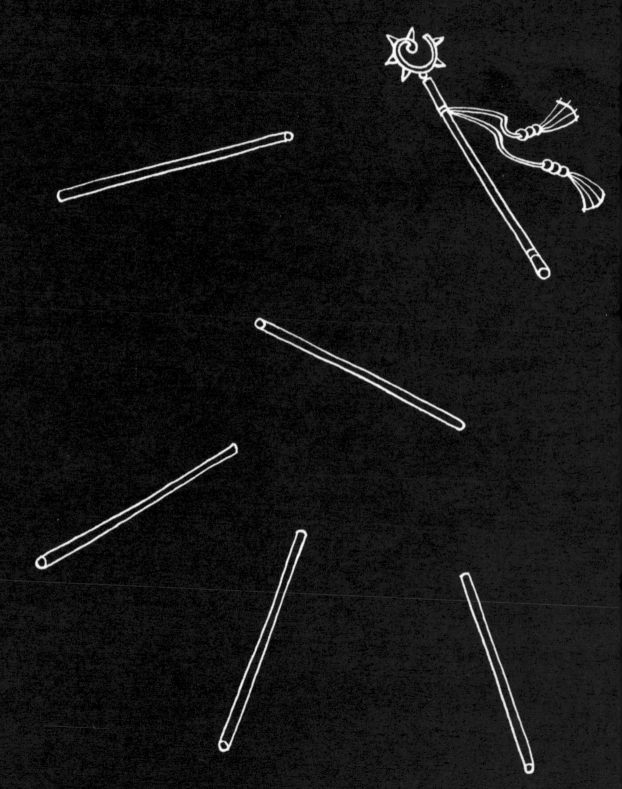